MW01094015

I'm Celibate, Now What?

*The Christian Woman's Guide to
Getting Satisfied Without Sex*

Latonya Jones

Tymm Publishing LLC
Columbia, SC

I'm Celibate, Now What?
The Christian Woman's Guide to Getting Satisfied Without Sex

Copyright © 2018 by Latonya Jones

The information shared in the book represents an experience lived through by the author. Any resemblance to actual persons, living or dead, or actual events is purely coincidental. The advice and strategies discussed may not be suitable for every situation.

Paperback ISBN: 978-1-7329902-0-3
Ebook ISBN: 978-1-7329902-1-0

Tymm Publishing LLC
701 Gervais St, Suite 150-185
Columbia, SC 29201

Editor: Felicia Murrell
Cover Design: Tywebbin Creations

Dedication

I dedicate this book to my children. Because of you, I am a better woman and a better mother. I pray that every generational curse, known and unknown, are destroyed over your lives, in Jesus name, and that he continues to grant me and every member of your support system with the wisdom, love, empathy, respect, resources, obedience, and protection needed so that you are able to live out God's ordained purpose for your lives. Love, Mom.

Acknowledgements

Many thanks to my family, friends, associates, church ladies, past and present co-workers, and supporters for the work, research, guidance, love, encouragement, and support, that has helped me to write this book. Thank You God, for granting me the grace to live through and learn from these experiences to be able to educate and ignite healing to this population of women across the world.

Table of Contents

Introduction

Women all over the world are desperately seeking their Boaz, their relationship goals, soulmates, life partners, and husbands. Social media has made it easy for the popularity of relationship experts, self-love ambassadors, pastors, and friends to use their platform to educate women on how to attract the man of your dreams. Sometimes this work, sometimes it doesn't. Often times, if you listen to these various genres of people at one time, the message can be very conflicting, creating anxiety and lack of encouragement.

Over time, you may fall prey to believing the epidemic that there is a shortage of men, or all men are dogs, or that you have to move to a new city in order to find a man. But what if the secret to finding a good man is through finding yourself? What if you find yourself and lose your man? What if you practice every rule identified by these self-love ambassadors and relationship experts only to discover that God's plan for you is to remain single? If you take away your quest to find or to be found by a man, would you still be satisfied with yourself?

Many women are practicing celibacy as their last result to attract a man. If you are living this lifestyle or considering this lifestyle, then you can agree that premarital sex oftentimes clouds your judgement, leaving you stuck in toxic, abusive, dead-end relationships with the illusion that disrespect, lack of support, and verbal/physical/or mental abuse is love. If you are successful to end these types of relationships, and then allow yourself a few months of being alone only to end up attracting another abusive, controlling, disrespectful partner, one has to ask, why is that? Unable to identify the answer, you join a church to seek healing and dedicate yourself to celibacy until you are married.

The problem is, you find yourself lonely and craving the companionship of a man. The only advice anyone can give you is to "pray about it," but you've prayed a million times already. God must have not gotten the memo! The good news is *I'm Celibate, Now What? - The Christian Woman's Guide to Being Satisfied Without Sex* was designed with you in mind. I'm here to share with you my personal journey on how I became celibate and what this journey has taught me thus far. Together, we will heal, encourage, and inspire others through our actions.

Chapter 1

In the Beginning

     Women enter celibacy for various reasons. For some, it was always taught and instilled in them as a little girl that they are not to have sex before marriage. For others, their sexual rights were compromised by a stranger, loved one, or a family member. Maybe you were married and now divorced or widowed but experiencing celibacy for the first time in your adult life. Maybe you are like me, entering celibacy as the result of a toxic relationship, heartbreak, and fed up with giving yourself to the wrong man. Regardless of when or why you decided to abstain from sex, this new life can be very challenging as you learn to control your emotions and to date the opposite sex without having sex.

     When I entered puberty, I was constantly told that sex before marriage was wrong. I was not given any reason for why it was wrong, I was simply told it was wrong. The way I was reared, you respect your elder and do as you were told. My elders told me, "Why would a guy marry the cow if he can get the milk for free?" When I was younger, I had no idea what that meant. Was I a cow? Who gave out free milk anyways?

Before my grandmother passed, I spent a lot of time at her house. I can remember crying to attend church with her. There was not much to do growing up and church was where you went to catch up on the happenings in the neighborhood, find out the latest gossip, and be entertained by the pastor. The point is, I did not grow up in a super-religious, holier than thou background. We believed in Jesus, loved the Lord, said our prayers, and that pretty much summed up my Christian experience.

When I enrolled in college, I was introduced to a whole new world. It was my first time away from home, alone. My parents, I'm sure with good intentions, dropped me off with what little belongings I had and instructed me to call home when necessary. The day had come that every teenager desperately longed for, I was officially *grown* or at least I thought. Reality settled in when I had no idea how to make a dollar out of fifteen cents. I needed to devise a plan and execute it fast.

Prior to my freshman year in college, I was sorta kinda in a relationship with this guy back home. We started off as friends. He was ending a relationship with his former partner, and I did not want to be his rebound. So, I allowed space and kept things casual until what they had was officially over. In the meantime, we spent lots of time over the phone watching television together, sharing stories about our day-to-day activities, and laughing at each other's jokes. In the spring of the following year, he asked me out again, stating that his prior relationship was officially over and it was safe to date. His ex, who had also moved on to another relationship, knew about us and gave her approval. She often visited us at work and hung out with both of us.

4

Our friendship was great so I figured our relationship would be even better. Never mind that I had no idea how to date. I was always told I should not have a boyfriend so I guess that's why it was never important to be educated on how to conduct a relationship with a guy. Prior to my first relationship, I had what my elders called *puppy-love* type relationships, nothing serious, just incidental relationships with the guys I interacted with at school. The general consensus was to wait until you were "grown" to start dating. When my friend and I started dating, I was a few weeks shy of my eighteenth birthday and leaving for college soon, pre-grown.

When I went away to college, the guy I was dating decided to enter the workforce in our hometown. The distance between us was relatively short, yet far apart for a pair of teenagers learning how to navigate the highways. He was the only connection I had to the normal life I previously lived. Instead of going out and getting to know the people I went to school with, I spent most of my time going to class or on the phone with my guy.

It wasn't long before we were professing our love for each other and transitioning into a more serious phase in our relationship. Eventually, the distance was putting a strain on our relationship because we couldn't see each other as often as we liked. What I did not know at the time, and later discovered, was his ex had ended her relationship with her boyfriend and the friendship between my guy and his ex had reignited. Nevertheless, I had no reason to be insecure about their relationship, at the time, as they were just *friends* and my guy and I appeared to be separated by distance yet solid in hearts.

Our relationship was very rocky during the months leading up to winter break. It was difficult to reach him by phone and when we did talk on the phone he was often tired after a long day of work. If I wanted to save what was left of our relationship, I had to step up in a major way. When I met him, he was not a virgin and although he said he didn't think about sex like that and assured this would not be a problem, I knew what I had to do in order to keep the relationship flourishing. Besides, we loved each other and we both knew we would one day marry each other. Why should we wait until marriage to have sex? Marriage seemed so far away. Neither one of us was in a position financially to purchase a home or rent an apartment, and love should not have to wait. It was time to eliminate any temptation and distractions between him and any additional females that was consuming his time and energy.

Shortly after giving him my virginity, I was heartbroken and single. He told me he could no longer trust me since I was attending college sixty miles away. How could that be? The day of our break up, I thought it was a joke. How did we transition from best friends who talked every day to having trust issues? I had never given him a reason not to trust me. I was available each and every time he called. I was aware that his ex was back in the picture, but I honestly thought they were just friends. I had no idea how much free time they were actually spending together.

I reasoned that perhaps he was under some type of stress at home or work and just needed time to calm down. The following morning, I was faced with the harsh reality of our breakup. We had developed a routine of him calling every morning before work and I didn't get a phone call from him that morning. I skipped class hoping he was just in a rush and would call during his fifteen-minute break. Nine hours passed and I knew his work day was done. With the exception of leaving my room to use the restroom and take a quick shower, I had stayed in my dorm all day waiting by the phone. I did not eat, did not attend class. I remained available for him, hoping this was a terrible dream.

For ninety plus days, I did this. Waiting by the phone, skipping out on meals and avoiding class, hoping he would call and tell me this was a very bad dream. Life without him was extremely unbearable. I felt as if I would die without a relationship with him. For the last year and a half, my entire world had revolved around him. I forgot how to live or cope without having a man in my life. After months and months in bed with little moving around, I developed bedsores. I had never had a bedsore before so I thought I was literally dying from his lack of involvement in my life. Somehow, I determined this was not the end and I could not go out like that. Instead of giving up hope and feeling sorry for myself, the bedsore became a sign that it was time to move on, physically and mentally.

During that brief transition of learning how to live without him, something terrible transpired within me. I equated his lack of love for my self-worth, somehow identifying how to love myself based on the love he had shown me. If he didn't love me, I resolved, then I must be unlovable. He had not found me worthy enough so I was unworthy. He did not care about me so I was undeserving of being cared for. I gave him my virginity, the most prized possession I had to offer a man, and he treated this occasion as if I was a customer in the drive-thru line at a fast food restaurant. He broke up with me and left me with a hideous explanation that made no logical sense. In return, I taught myself to hate me. Obviously I wasn't good enough. Something was wrong with me and he left me with no explanation and no opportunity to improve myself and meet his needs.

I developed low self-esteem. I felt like damaged goods, unworthy to be loved. I struggled with understanding why he said he loved me if he didn't really love me. Why would he abandon me like that after months of being a part of each other lives? He hadn't disregarded his last relationship in the same manner, so what was wrong with me? What did I do wrong? Clearly something must be wrong with me for this guy to just decide without warning that he wanted to end the relationship. I was too embarrassed to reach out for help. Honestly, I had lost contact with all of my high school friends because my life was consumed with entertaining him. And, I had yet to make any friends at college because my time was consumed with waiting by the phone anticipating his call. There I was, isolated, depressed, lonely, and too embarrassed to reach out for help.

As one semester transitioned into the next, I slowly began to reintroduce myself to society. Admittedly, I often walked around like a zombie, wandering around out of place, desperately seeking to belong and gain acceptance. Even though I did not know anyone on campus, I felt like everyone knew my story, which made me feel embarrassed and ashamed even more. I decided to create a new normal. Things back home were financially strained, and I obtained a part time job at a mall department store to somewhat support myself. This kept me busy and kept my mind off of my ex. Having a job gave me the opportunity to get out of my room and meet people who were not attached to school.

8

When the time came to prepare for summer break, I contemplated how things would go back at home without having my ex around over the summer. All of my high school friends had moved away and were living new lives in different cities. With nothing to do in the small town where we lived, I worked it out with my manager to commute two days a week and continue my part time job.

I called my mom to determine which day she would pick me up from school based on her work schedule, and she suggested I call my ex. Nearly six months had passed since the last time we spoke. I couldn't just pick up the phone and ask if he could help move me home from school, but my mom was unaware that we had broken up and that was not the time to tell her. I had no desire to relive the past six months of an experience I wasn't ready to talk about. Unsure of what would happen, I took a leap of faith and made the bold decision to give him a call.

To my surprise, he answered. He asked, "What's wrong," as if he knew I needed a favor. I explained it was time for me to come home for summer break and asked if he would be willing to help me move back home, and he agreed.

He set a date and time and showed up as promised with a few extra hands to help load boxes and bags into his car. When I got into his car, he introduced me to his new set of friends as his "girl". Although I was confused, something about that moment healed me. The hole he had forged in my heart instantly stitched up. He dropped me off at home and promised he would call me later. Sure enough, I received a phone call later on that night. We laughed and talked all night and within a matter of moments, I had my best friend back. I was still confused about our break up, but he never provided any additional details as to why we could not be together. The last thing I wanted to do was ask why we broke up because I didn't want to lose him again. He did subtly confess that he had made a mistake letting me go and that he never stopped loving me. I accepted this moment of reconciliation. If you love something let it go. If it comes back, it was meant to be...right?

That summer went down in history as the best summer of our relationship. We spent practically every day together. On my days off, I would visit his job and bring him lunch. On weekends, we would travel and go out on dates. On Sundays, we went to church together and spent quiet time in parks after dinner. While apart, we talked on the phone until one of us drifted off to sleep. He would call every morning before leaving for work and every evening when he got off. This honeymoon phase lasted throughout my sophomore year. He visited campus often and Saturday date nights were still a thing.

By the time I was a junior in college, we were sharing our first apartment together. Our relationship still seemed stronger and living together only increased that. I had heard that "shacking" was "wrong," so I agreed to move in with him if it was going to lead to marriage after graduation. It was our first time with shared financial responsibility, and it was good to practice how things would be once we were married. We were paying bills together, grocery shopping, and still having date nights. He was very supportive in helping me reach my graduation goals and checked in daily to make sure I was attending class.

I had purchased an affordable car to get back and forth to campus, and he took on the role of making sure my car was serviced and always had gas in the tank. The security and comfort I felt from him being the man of the house allowed me to trust that he loved me. The more he loved me, the more I loved me and as long as he loved me, nothing else mattered.

Chapter 2

Trouble In Paradise

As I entered my senior year, the excitement and anticipation of finishing school was very high. I failed most of my classes during freshman year and had to attend summer school and take nearly twenty credits each semester of my senior year in order to graduate on time. He felt responsible for me not performing my best in my freshmen year, so he agreed that I would work less hours in my senior year and he would pick up the extra financial responsibility. I thought that was very responsible and mature of him and one of the many testimonies of how great things were between us. I hope and prayed things would be this great forever. But you know what they say, all good things eventually come to an end.

Occasionally, we would spend the weekend in our hometown, attend church and have Sunday dinner with our family. One routine Sunday, while visiting our hometown to go to church with my parents, he developed an unexpected attitude. When we left each other's presence Friday night, things between us were normal. Saturday, we were doing individual activities to prepare for our week ahead, and because of our busy weekend schedule, I assumed his attitude was due to a lack of communication.

Feeling somewhat responsible for his attitude, I retraced the events that had happened since we last saw each other. I thought perhaps I had neglected him in some way with my running around, handling household chores. In an urgent attempt to diffuse the situation, I apologized profusely. He told me if I wanted to make things right, I would have to come pick him up for church because he didn't feel like driving to my parents' house. A relationship is about compromise, right? So, I went to pick him up. When I arrived at his house, he was not ready for church. I felt embarrassed for being played for a fool and lashed out at him in rage and anger.

I later realized that my rage was the response he was looking for so he could blame me for that moment. After a violent argument and days of not talking to each other, he revealed that his attitude was because he was unsure how to tell me he had a three month old baby with another woman. The feeling I experienced freshman year during our first break up returned. Only this time, adding to the embarrassment factor, everybody in both of our families knew of his betrayal. I could not afford the level of depression I had endured previously in my freshman year, so I drowned myself in work, internships, and school projects, doing whatever I could to keep my mind off him, his baby, and the betrayal.

At night, it seemed as if the world stopped. I had trouble sleeping. I spent most of my time recalculating where I went wrong in the relationship. Trying to identify how he found the time to cheat on me when we were living and spending time together. After I tired myself out ruminating about all the ways he betrayed me, I started missing him. I was used to lying next to him and recapping my day while snuggling in his arms. I was used to hearing about his day at work and listening to his corny jokes.

Everything that I loved about him, I began to hate about him because he was sharing all that I loved about him with another woman. I had constant thoughts of comparison. Who is she? How does she look? Is she prettier than me? Better than me? What made her so special that he wanted to create a baby with her? I went from feeling as if I was the luckiest girl in the world to feeling like the most foolish girl in the world. How many other women had he cheated with? Why didn't I see any of the signs? What about me made him want to betray me? I grew frustrated trying to figure out when he had the time to cheat. If he kept that a secret, what else was he keeping secret?

I became embittered and angry towards men, even more so towards women who appeared confident, boastful, and bragged about being able to have any man they wanted. Those were the type of women I imagined ruined relationships, or so I thought. I even felt betrayed by his family for keeping his secret. I thought they were my family too. We spent holidays together and enjoyed random family moments together. Why would they hide his cheating from me and not give me a small clue? I was angry at his friends because they knew all about his double lifestyle and no one warned me. I thought his friends were my friends. We all hung out together, went bowling together, played pool together. How could they do that to me? Overall, I was angry at everyone connected to him.

I spent months crying and avoiding him. He agreed to move back home but would randomly appear at my job or at the apartment without permission. During our break, his grandmother would call to "check in on me" and I thought that was the sweetest, slickest move ever to show that he still loved me. Over time, I allowed him to come back around. Apologizing yet again for the damage he had done. But from that moment on, our relationship was never the same. I could no longer trust him and my insecurities were at an all-time high. I questioned everything he did and everywhere he went. I basically became a private investigator, calculating the miles on his car, checking phone logs, following him to the barbershop and other places he spent his free time. This was tiring and time consuming, so I allowed him to move back into our apartment. I felt if we were going to give this relationship another chance, I had to keep an eye on him.

The romantic time that we use to spend together was now spent in awkward silence. Our date nights diminished because I was embarrassed to be with him in public. I remained in the dark about who the other woman was and felt vulnerable to her. What if she walked up and attacked me? I felt like everyone was making a mockery out of our relationship since I was the last to know he was cheating. Even though I was still in love with the familiarity of having him around, the guy I fell in love with was no longer available. The more I stayed in the relationship, the more embarrassed I was to be with him. I felt as if people judged me for continuing to date him, and I did not want to publicly be labeled as a fool for taking back a cheater.

I wish I could say this was the first and last time he cheated. I thought sex was the problem. If we had more sex, would he stop cheating? Nope. Not at all, then sex started to feel like a chore. Something I had to do in order to be with him. Love and intimacy was no longer in the picture. When we were not having sex, I interrogated and we argued, eventually becoming physically violent. As time passed, I grew weak and tired. There was no way I could defeat him, physically or mentally. One night after sex, I told him I was leaving the state to start over in a new city shortly after graduation where no one would be able to connect me to him or the embarrassment he caused. I knew that distancing myself from him was the only way I could restore sanity and safety back into my life. We both began to plan in private for how we would live our lives after my graduation.

Chapter 3

Welcome to the Real World

Twelve months after the birth of his first child, I became a proud college graduate. He attended my graduation like he promised, and I felt I at least owed him some type of gratitude for continuing to maintain the household while I was going to school so I could accomplish my goal. After graduating, I had no job, my student loan repayment was about to begin, and we discovered I was eight weeks pregnant with his second child. Consumed with monitoring and tracking his life, I had failed to monitor and track my birth control or thoroughly plan my exit strategy for moving on from the relationship I no longer desired to be in. In the back of my mind, I wanted to believe his cheating was a one-time event that we could get past, but I did not know how to get past it. I kept wanting to know why he cheated on me. He had no explanation but appeared to be remorseful, though he was always remorseful after a major disagreement. And that made me question the sincerity of his remorse. Was it just an act to keep me in a relationship with him?

Being pregnant left me confused. I was excited to be a mom but terrified to bring a baby into our dysfunction. I was not sure if he was going to leave or stick around. I had no idea the type of father he would be because he sucked at being a boyfriend. When I told him I was pregnant, he appeared to be excited which was somewhat of a relief. He continued to pay all the bills in our apartment and gave me money for routine hair and nail appointments to contribute to rebuilding my self-esteem since his last stunt really broke me. I was stressed and fragile, my hair was falling out and I doubted myself constantly. It was a miracle I even graduated considering the amount of emotional duress.

Pregnancy with him was not how I imagined. On TV, pregnant women were spoiled during pregnancy: feet, back, and belly rubs, babymoons, baby showers, and cute little birth announcements. I barely saw him during the pregnancy because he worked a tremendous amount of overtime. Tired from working so much, sex was almost nonexistent. Not that it bothered me, I was huge as a whale and felt very unattractive. The most romantic moment during my pregnancy was the few times he attended doctor appointments, the time spent in the delivery room, and the way I observed him bonding with the baby during rare moments of rest. I know I should not complain because after all, he was there, which was more than what some young mothers in complicated relationships with their child(ren)'s father got.

During my pregnancy, he would randomly try to convince me that no other woman would come between us. That he was done playing around and things would be different this time because we had a family. Thirty days after the birth of our child, I found a telephone number in his wallet. I simply could not endure another heartbreak of this magnitude while learning how to parent. Not again! When I discovered the number in his wallet, our argument became so violent and reckless that our families got involved. It took long enough, but I finally realized he would never change. He had embarrassed me for the last time. Enough was enough.

Several years passed and our relationship took on an abusive, toxic pattern. We would take time off and then reunite after months of being apart. It was like we could not live without each other. As painful as the heartbreak was, something felt right about being with him. Each time, I was led to believe he had thought about and changed his negative behaviors only to end up disappointed and broken for believing his lies. Our relationship became a predictable routine. We would make up and be so in love then I would discover another woman. We would fight and break up. Repeat. Each time I took him back, I felt more worthless. I knew deep down inside that I deserved better, but this was the only guy I knew. Perhaps if these other women could understand he was taken, maybe they would stop coming in between us.

Our child was two years old when he finally proposed. That engagement did not last and he proposed again when our child was four years old. I wanted to believe that he had outgrown the cheating and the lies. Both times I thought, *finally, the moment I've been waiting for!* But deep down, something was not right. My family was not thrilled or supportive of our engagement. It was one of those, I need to see it to believe it type of things. And each time I put on my engagement ring, my ring finger itched. I often had dreams of the diamonds falling out. I spiritually knew this was not the guy God wanted me to marry and if I did marry him, God would not be a part of this union.

I remember asking God to show me a sign that I was not supposed to marry this guy. I wanted more

21

than a dream of diamonds falling out of a ring. I wanted more than a family feud. I wanted more than feeling miserable and alone although I was in a relationship. I wanted visual evidence that he was not the one. By that time, we had entered the age of social media and one night while scrolling, everything made sense. I was lurking around on social media, not sure what I was looking for, but I was searching. One profile led to another and another profile led me to another profile. I finally came across a profile where my fiancé was hugged up with another woman. Judging by her profile, these two were traveling together and dining out in some of the same cities and restaurants he had taken me too. Everything he had done with me, he was now doing with her. To make matters worse, she appeared to be a version of my younger self. So here I was, aging and taking care of his child by myself while being led to believe he was working overtime so he could save for our wedding.

Unlike the past, when I found out about another woman and he assured me she was just a friend and nothing serious was going on between them, this time things were different. He had disregarded me as his fiancée and painted a picture of me to the other woman as the bitter, jealous ex-girlfriend or the crazy baby momma that could not leave him alone. The more I tried to prove to her that I was his *main chick,* the more I appeared to be crazy. He was the liar. He was the aggressor. It was not long before his new girlfriend and her family ganged together, justifying his betrayal towards me. I was accused of being crazy, a bad mother, a bad girlfriend, and an evil person who was attempting to ruin his life.

Months went by before I talked with or saw him again. And the thing I dreaded most happened, I was officially a single parent. To be completely vulnerable, I *was* a bitter baby momma. My child no longer had a father and I was angry he had left us. I was unable to financially support my child the way I wanted. I barely made enough money to take care of myself. I knew I could not take care of a child on my income alone. I wish I had another adjective to use, but the abandonment and mental abuse my ex perpetrated upon me made me angry, and now he was doing that to our child. I had to grieve the loss of my love and our relationship and then take on the pain my child was experiencing. Initially, I thought this was just another phase, that it would play out for a few months and I would have my family back, that he would come around.

He eventually did, but it was not to be a father to our child. He wanted me to be the side chick, as long as I didn't tell the main chick about our interactions. At first, I disagreed. I use to be number one, now he was asking me to be number two? But it hurt to have my child question why Daddy was never around. Why Daddy did not visit the school today or take him to the county fair or for ice cream after church on Sundays? I could only endure so much pain from seeing my child ache for the love of his father and wonder why his dad no longer had a relationship with him. It was not long before my ex made me believe his absence and betrayal were my fault. If I would agree to this demotion, stay off social media, and be his side chick, I could have the family I always wanted. He led me to believe my problem was that I cared too much about what people think. That I should be happy with the life he had provided for me and not interact with associates on social media who negatively influenced me or told me that our relationship was toxic. Our latest arrangement was brief. I no longer felt like sharing or waiting by the phone for him to return my phone calls.

After ten plus years in the relationship, I finally severed my ties with him for good. I stopped having sex with him, changed my phone number, disconnected my involvement with his family and stopped believing the lies. There were moments I still yearned for him, but I knew I had to fight through these withdrawals. I grew tired of crying, tired of being alone, tired of having to share my love with him, tired of feeling less than. I contributed my awareness to a new church I had started attending. I have no idea what led me to the church, but I knew I was broken inside. The type of brokenness that surgery could not fix. These undiagnosed issues on the inside of my heart were leaking toxicity everywhere. I needed a change and church was the only way I knew how to fix it.

Chapter 4

As Within, so Without

The universal law, "As within, so without," tells us that we cannot achieve our purpose or our goals in life until we achieve harmony between our physical and spiritual world. What is going on inside of us is a reflection of what will happen outside of us.

I returned to church hoping that church would fix my problem. And in some aspects, it did. Things at my new church were great. I met great people, volunteered, and became actively involved. I had been abstaining from sex for several years, but something was not quite right with me, and at the time I didn't know how to verbalize it. On the surface, I was lonely, still very much depressed, and struggled with connecting with others. Overall, I was not satisfied. Eventually, I went to the only medicine I knew would heal me.

A man.

I believed being in a relationship with a man would help fill the void of loneliness. Hanging out at church was cool, but those people did not come home with me every night. I did not have any "church friends," and most of them were married, in committed relationships, or outgoing enough to create meaningful friendships.

Shortly after I expressed my dream to the universe of wanting to be in a relationship, I met a guy. He was older and I assumed more mature. On our first date, we laughed and enjoyed each other's company. He worked out of town and came to visit often. While away, we spent hours over the phone discussing goals for our relationship, if we would have more children and where we would live. He included me in his future plans and made himself available to me around our hectic work schedules. I was starting a new career and he was very supportive. In a lot of ways, he reminded me of my first relationship. It was easy to love him and fall into a routine because he was doing every good thing my last guy did.

There was one aspect of his life that slightly concerned me. He had been married before and had vowed to never marry again. In the back of my inexperienced mind, I thought I could change that. He told me often I was unlike any other woman he had ever dealt with. He pointed out qualities and traits in me that I did not know I had, and this made me feel really special. He helped restore every insecurity I had about myself. If I did not like my weight, we worked out together. If I felt insecure financially, he gave me money and taught me how to save. If I was having a bad day, he sent me flowers.

Would I be the next ex-wife? At least I would finally meet my goal of being somebody's wife. Nevertheless, I wanted to enjoy the moment, whatever may come of it. Being around him was fun and exciting. He was the first guy I connected with since ending the relationship with my high school sweetheart. I told him I was celibate, and I gave him the same spiel I had given my previous partner. I was not engaging in sexual activity unless he was serious that one day we would marry.

He explained his four-year plan and described how I fit into it. I was still hesitant because I had been down this road before. A guy with a plan, included me in his plan, but never met the goal. I had been led to believe he was going to work every day accomplishing goals for "us" while he engaged in secret relationships. In an effort to not appear bitter or heartbroken (because I had convinced myself that I was over that life and the heartbreak that came with it), I decided to move forward into a relationship with this guy.

Everything about this guy helped me understand why my last relationship did not work. This guy made me feel different. He always made sure I felt special. Sex with him was not a job or something I had to do to keep him from other women. He introduced me to a new experience and I converted that new experience into an expression of love for me. Spoiler alert: my fairytale would soon come to an end. About six months into the relationship, I started having dreams of our relationship failing. Strange women approached me in my dreams to inform me about his infidelities.

Hesitant, I called up my guy and told him my dream. I had made the mistake of telling him all the sordid details about my last relationship, and he convinced me that insecurity from my past relationship was trying to rear its head in my current relationship. This is how he was able to tell me confidently that my dreams were a reflection of my relationship insecurities.

One day, as I was preparing to meet him for dinner, a feeling of grief overwhelmed me. Grief represents loss, and though I was not sure how I would lose him, I felt that one day he would no longer be a part of my life. I prayed to God that nothing would happen to him or our relationship, thinking perhaps this was insecurity from the last relationship sneaking in. For the first time in a long time, I felt secure and happy. I wasn't alone anymore. I woke up to "good morning" texts and random phone calls throughout the day to let me know he was thinking about me. I had someone to share my life and accomplishments with. This man had changed my life for the better, and I did not think my heart could suffer another loss.

I prayed and asked God to release me from the anxiety so I could continue to enjoy my relationship. Later that day, I shared with him my fear of losing him. He reassured me that he would never leave, proclaiming me his peace from the craziness of the world. He even promised we would be engaged within two years. As we approached the culmination of our first year of dating, every insecurity I had about him waned. If I could tolerate another year, we would be engaged and soon married and all my anxiety and insecurity would be alleviated.

To celebrate our one-year anniversary, we agreed it was time to meet the parents. He had spent time with other members of my extended family, but because of all the drama in my last relationship, I was hesitant to bring another man around my family. I personally vowed to never hurt my family that way again.

We spoke over the phone and planned the exchange. Would it be grand? A party or a vacation? Or something low-key like a barbeque or a dinner? The more we planned, the more my anxiety heightened. I knew something was not right about this relationship. Because of my experience with loneliness, I convinced myself anxiety was better than being alone.

Two weeks before our plan was to unfold, I discovered he was involved with his ex-wife. Confused, furious and faced with another failed relationship, I lashed out at him. He worked overtime to prove the legality of his divorce to me, telling me he was only with her so she could help him accomplish his financial goals. I was not buying it. I was done.

Although they were legally divorced, their community of friends and family still considered them a married couple. I had already been shamed into being a bad mother, a bitter baby momma, the crazy delusional ex-girlfriend, the woman who would do anything to keep her man, the last thing I needed was to be called a home-wrecker. The embarrassment, abandonment, and feeling of defeat was too heavy to bear. I had spent years in a relationship filled with trauma that left me with low self-esteem, unable to trust my judgement and riddled with fear of abandonment. That relationship taught me that each time an offense occurred, we had to start over with building trust. I was older, and I did not have another ten plus years to invest in stopping and starting over with another guy. I desired to be married, sooner rather than later. It was best if I ended the relationship.

Chapter 5

To Steal, Kill, and Destroy

Within weeks, I was back to being lonely and depressed. I was over the entire dating thing. Manipulation was at an all-time high in the dating world, and I simply did not want to invest my mind and emotions into another relationship. Men were using women for financial gain and women were using men for social status, free meals, and whatever other needs they wanted fulfilled. It appeared nobody loved each other anymore and the average marriage was considered a business arrangement or a means to gain social status.

I was angry at myself for breaking my celibacy agreement. I was angry at God for not sending me the relationship I knew I deserved. I was angry at my first boyfriend for breaking my heart and abandoning me to be a single mother. I was angry and bitter at everyone who appeared to be living the life I wanted. In short, I was mad at the world. Relationships and lies were a thing of the past for me, but I still felt like a relationship was the only thing that would cure my pain.

Determined not to ride this pain, I ran across the perfect distraction one night while grocery shopping. A certified player, he was young and charismatic with the sex appeal to match. He had nothing going for himself—no goals, dreams, desires, or ambitions to do anything other than drive all the gas out of your car while you were at work. He was the type to cook all your groceries, eat all the snacks you bought for the kids, and call you on your way home to demand an allowance. He was very good with providing unsolicited encouragement in the form of gassing you up with the perfect amount of self-worth during random moments when you felt resentful for even entertaining a guy like this. With no desire to enter a relationship with him, he was the perfect distraction and pain reliever from the broken heart I had no idea how to heal.

Eleven months into this uncommitted relationship, I started encountering several problems, or attacks, whichever you prefer. I guess I deserved it, I'd been on a rebellious streak for nearly three years. I thought life was good because I had someone I could sit on the phone and vent to. He was not a consistent partner, but at least I was not alone all of the time. We coasted along in this complicated situation-ship until the day my menstrual cycle was later than usual. Assuming it was just stress and the antidepressants I had recently been prescribed, I was too focused on my problems to even consider being pregnant at this point.

For years, it seemed as if I was just a sex doll to the guys I was in a relationship with. To them, I was an object to satisfy their emotionless sexual desire while I was under the impression that we were bonding and growing mutually as a couple. I grew tired of allowing my emotions to get caught up in a guy who did not feel the same way about me as I felt about him. I was tired of not being able to control

32

when I gave up my body, and I knew somewhere deep inside, I was worth more than casual sex or years of being in a committed one-sided relationship while my partner sexed anybody and everything. I wanted to be in control of my emotions, my feelings, my heart, and my vagina. Even though this guy and I was not in a relationship, I felt as if we had a general understanding and mutual benefit. He was using me for whatever his personal reasons were and I was using him to be healed of loneliness.

A baby was not part of the plan. With all of the financial, emotional, and spiritual problems I was encountering, having a baby at this point in my life would be a total disaster, especially by a guy I barely knew. I had spent years struggling as a single parent, caring for my current child with the financial, physical, and mental absence of that child's father. I knew I never wanted to put another child through that type of torment ever again. With the current guy, I always knew in the back of my mind that our relationship was temporary. I just didn't expect to end up being a single mother with a high-risk pregnancy.

As I reflect upon the moment I discovered I was pregnant, I remember feeling the lowest I had ever felt in my adult life. Being pregnant was akin to hitting rock bottom. They say that rock bottom is the solid foundation on which you can rebuild your life, and my life was definitely broken. My finances were in shambles, my current child was acting out, and the relationship with my family was extremely strained.

The scriptures say, "The thief comes only to steal and kill and destroy. I came that they may have life and have it abundantly" (John 10:10, ESV). I was so far away from God, I could barely pray and often wanted to die. I was struggling to take care of my current child. He was spiraling out of control and it seemed as if no one could reel him back in. I was struggling to take care of myself and was in danger of losing everything I had worked so hard to obtain. This guy made it clear that if I wanted to be in a relationship with him, I would have to be his provider and I simply could not afford to be his provider. Broke and afraid, I called an abortion clinic.

I was already a sinner, I thought to myself as I called the clinic. I knew God would forgive me but how would I ever forgive myself? I felt like a rape victim. I did not consent to getting pregnant by him, so why should I have to be connected to this event for the rest of my life by birthing his baby? Meanwhile, he gets to go on with his life, finding other victims to supply his lifestyle while impregnating them if they do not comply with his request. If he could be free, so should I. I had it all figured out. I would abort the baby, repent, stop fornicating, and live my best life while trying to revamp it.

When the operator answered the phone and went over the financial details, I did my best to remain confident that I was making the best decision. I guess she could hear the uncertainty in my voice as she went over financial and insurance options. I did not have insurance and I did not have any money, but I requested to be transferred to the scheduling department. I ended up leaving a voicemail, requesting a call back so I could schedule a time to abort this baby.

I was struggling financially to take care of the current members of my household, my child was having behavioral problems, and we had legal troubles to worry about. It was too much to handle. I was afraid to tell anyone in my family because I felt I had already caused them enough heartache and stress.

I did eventually muster up enough strength to call the baby's dad, hoping he would have a change of heart and talk me out of aborting the baby. He did not answer so I left a voicemail telling him that I was scheduling an abortion and that I did not want anything to do with him after the baby was aborted. The next twenty-four hours following that voicemail were the longest twenty-four hours of my life. I contemplated how I would live with myself if I killed a baby because of a mistake I made. Whatever this child was destined to be, it did not deserve the consideration of an abortion.

I called the one guy I was good at communicating with, the guy that I was in a relationship with before meeting the father of my second child. He was older and more experienced with life, but despite our differences, he was a good communicator and had always been able to help me reason. I truly believed our relationship would have been better if we had remained friends and never engaged in sex. This was our first conversation since the breakup, and I was completely vulnerable while explaining how I ended up in this mess. Thankfully, he knew my character enough to know that I would not be able to live with myself if I killed the baby.

I did not schedule the abortion and stayed away from the guy who made me question doing such a thing. Throughout the pregnancy, I was unable to connect with the baby because of the drama I was in. Although I had waived the option to abort, I continued to resent being pregnant. I resented it so much, I waited until I was twelve weeks to visit the doctor, hoping the baby would abort itself.

On my first visit, I found out there was excess fluid on the baby's neck and I would need to see a specialist. I thought this was karma for wanting the baby to die. But once I heard the heartbeat, this illusion became a reality and I knew my job was to protect this child. The excess fluid behind the neck became the least of our worries as the doctor expressed concern about my blood count levels. I had always struggled with anemia, and thought it was no big deal. Nothing some iron pills couldn't handle.

I was praying it was not HIV. To cut the suspense, I was told that I was a genetic carrier for something called Spinal Muscular Atrophy or SMA. SMA is a disease that affects the muscular strength in your body by impacting the motor nerve cells in the spinal cord. This can affect a person's ability to walk, eat, or even breathe, and there was only one way to know if my child would be impacted by the disease. The father of the baby had to come in for testing.

The genetics counselor urged me to contact the child's father. It was crucial for determining best practices in utero to care for the child. I knew contacting him would trigger me and I was desperately trying to generate healing in my life. But, for the sake of my unborn baby, I called the father and left a voicemail explaining the seriousness of the disease and how important it was for him to be tested. He immediately returned my call. Feigning concern for the baby's health and my emotional state, he agreed to be tested. However, when the genetic counselor gave him a call, he declined. I was numb, there was no feeling left inside to become angry. I knew it was a mistake calling him. I felt like I had betrayed myself by believing he would agree to anything that required him to take accountability for this baby. I had no choice but to leave the situation up to God. If my baby was meant to live, yet again, God would provide him the strength necessary for survival.

In the meantime, I stopped going to doctor appointments and medical exams because I could not bear the stress of sitting around, waiting for more bad news.

By the time I was six months pregnant, my stomach is getting bigger and I figured this baby was not going to abort itself. I needed to tell my family I was pregnant. I requested they not ask me any details because being pregnant was humiliating enough. I felt like an embarrassment to my family and an even bigger embarrassment to myself.

Everyone in my family was married. My nieces and nephews were conceived within marriage. I was the only dysfunctional sister with out of wedlock children by multiple fathers, constantly bringing drama to my family. I had judged myself in every possible shape and form and beaten myself up mercilessly regarding my personal failures. I knew there was no further judgement or pain my family could offer when I shared my news with them. It was time to release myself of this guilt and shame and begin working towards the healthy emotions I needed to parent this child.

When I told my family I was pregnant, something inside shifted. I was surrounded by the love and support that I was missing all along. I began praying the baby would live and not die because I knew he would be a blessing to our family. I resumed prenatal appointments, eating as healthy as possible, and most importantly, I restored my relationship with God.

Chapter 6

The Great Awakening

At the time I decided to share my experience in a book, I was twenty-eights months into my latest round of celibacy. I had unsuccessfully practiced celibacy several times in the past. I would go two years then relapse, four years and then relapse. What damaged my soul even more was I was portraying myself as a Christian, but I was misrepresenting God. I had come to somewhat accept what others thought of me, but what mattered most was how I looked in God's eye. For me, this was my great awakening.

I was filled with personal guilt, conviction, and needed redemption through the salvation that Jesus Christ provided. I'm sure there are some out there who believe I was never celibate at all and was being a fraud for Jesus. It was never my intent to misrepresent the kingdom of God in that manner. I judged myself and was consumed with how others perceived me, which lead me to ask myself, "Am I celibate because I'm too busy to have sex? Am I celibate for real this time? Am I going all the way with this commitment to celibacy regardless if God blesses me with a husband or not?"

What I did know was that I no longer wanted to get trapped in a pregnancy by another guy I barely knew. I did not want to bring any more fatherless children into this world. And a low body count of sexual partners was very important to me. To minimize the self-doubt, I decided to focus on the facts.

I had not engaged in any sexual activity since my baby was conceived and my heart was pure towards the plans I believed God had for me. Not to mention, being a single parent of two children demanded all of my attention, sex should have been the last thing on my mind. I decided I needed a husband, and I needed one fast. Even with my children around, I was tired of being alone. But I felt that being in the company of men would put me back in the situation I was already in, single with children. I knew something different needed to be done in my life.

I reevaluated my life to determine why celibacy had not worked for me in the past. I studied women in my family, women on social media, even my female co-workers, observing the conditions that led them to marriage. Some women had multiple children by multiple partners. Some women did not know how to cook, manage a household, or have good financial practices. Some women ran the streets and partied/went clubbing every weekend. Yet, most of these women were married. Some women were physically unattractive and still managed to land a husband. Judging by what I observed, I knew I was more than qualified to be someone's wife. What was my problem?

During my pregnancy, the doctor wanted to know my birth control plan. Because I had been diagnosed with pre-eclampsia, he felt it was not safe for me to get pregnant again until I could control my high blood pressure. I declined birth control knowing that I was recommitting to a celibate lifestyle. When the doctor cleared me to have sex again, that's when the real challenge began.

Some nights, after the kids were asleep, I scrolled social media, looking at happy and in love couples. I couldn't help but wonder when my time was coming. Was celibacy really the way to go? I knew several couples who had engaged in premarital sex and still married. I only knew of one couple who were virgins prior to marriage, and I didn't know of any couples who chose celibacy prior to marriage.

I joined celibacy groups on social media looking for support, but the truth is, those types of groups lacked support. In my opinion, the groups were filled with moderately angry women who used social media to brag about how long they had been celibate or to complain about how men did not want to date celibate women. Most celibacy dating groups were filled with married men pretending to be single, preying on gullible celibate Christian women. A few celibate dating groups were more geared toward women and men ministering to each other about the roles of a husband and wife, but when I asked for success stories, no information was provided.

Being celibate and single, I have learned more women are looking to be validated by a husband than not. The unspoken rule of thumb tends to be: if you are single, something must be wrong with you. If you are celibate for less than five years, then you are not seriously celibate. If you are celibate for more than twenty years, something definitely must be wrong with you because it shouldn't take that long for God to bring you a husband.

If you are married, then your life is complete. Society has so many unspoken rules that if you are not confident in God's plan for your life, you can easily become a victim of self-induced low self-esteem, comparing your life to someone else who appears to have it all together. The very thing I was doing, judging whether a married person was worthy of marriage, was the reason why I was unsatisfied with being celibate. I worshipped the idea of having a husband and based on an outward appearance, I judged why others were unqualified to have a husband.

I decided celibacy was not a race given to the swift, so I chose not to focus on the length of time I was celibate. I needed to learn how to love myself while trusting that God's love for me was enough. I knew I wanted to grow further in my spiritual life so I could stop being in bondage to my flesh. I knew I needed to heal from the underlying mental issues that convinced me I was not good enough. Most importantly, I needed to heal from past traumas and abuse that were lying dormant inside of me.

The deficiency within myself caused me to seek approval from a certain type of man which I craved and idolized in a toxic manner. Once I attracted these particular guys and established a relationship, I believed the lie that I was worthless or invaluable if I did not remain attached to the guy. Whenever a toxic relationship ended, the emptiness inside of me was so profound, and I could not imagine a reality without that person. Used to relationships being fueled by drama and chaos, I had no idea what a healthy person or relationship looked like.

Being in an abusive relationship robs you of your creative energy, your time, and your peace. Most women fail to connect to the purpose of a painful relationship, lacking the accountability skills required to take ownership for attracting toxicity into our lives.

During the time I spent in celibate social media groups, it appeared that women from all walks of life was desperately duplicating the prayer of a popular pop singer in order to obtain a wealthy, respectable husband. I'd like to think that perhaps in addition to prayer, she was able to identify what she did and did not deserve. She took the time to identify what was broken inside of her and sought professional counseling or engaged self-guided healing techniques to correct the negative deficiencies inside of her.

Once this was accomplished, the singer exuded a certain level of confidence and vibrated at a higher frequency where a healthy, desirable man was able to notice her. He then wanted to protect her peace and existence and felt it was beneficial to marry her. This is my interpretation of what happened or at least what a healthy relationship with self that leads to the perfect fairytale or marriage/relationships should look like.

I can't make any guarantees, but I believe I have the formula through my self-guided healing that is beneficial to anyone woman transitioning from a toxic relationship into a lifestyle of celibacy. Maybe you were not in a toxic relationship but you are single, newly celibate, and unsatisfied. Abstaining from sex is only half the battle. While participating in social media groups advocating celibacy, I noticed a lot of women struggled with how to live a fulfilled life while abstaining from sex. Nearly all of them complained about being "lonely" which represented some type of issues with abandonment.

For some women in these groups, the length of time they were celibate made them superior to someone who was just starting out. This type of mentality is not a healthy mindset. We all need encouragement no matter where we are in our celibacy. How long a woman has been celibate should not determine her worth or "qualify" her for a husband.

As I participated in various social media groups for celibacy, I discovered similar profiles of celibate women:

Women like Karen who has been celibate for seventy-five years and is believing God for her husband. Meanwhile, Karen only goes to church and work and all the men in her church are married and when she is approached by a man, she refuses to give out her phone number because she is waiting for God to bring her a man since all of the men of the world are full of game.

Next, there are women like Lisa. Lisa was celibate for six months and met her husband within ninety days of being celibate. Newly married, she shares beautiful photos of their elaborate wedding that occurred last weekend. Now fresh off her honeymoon, for $2000.00, she's ready to sign you up and teach you exclusive secrets on how she leveled up, started her home based business, and married the man of her dreams.

Women are either discouraged by stories like Karen or unable to financially afford Lisa's secret to success. My objective for this book is to put an end to the stigma that you have to spend your life savings listening to someone else's secrets to success or be miserable waiting for Mr. Right to appear with a sign on his forehead saying he is Mr. Right. Most importantly, regardless of how you embarked on your personal journey to celibacy, you will be equipped with advice to activate a life of living satisfied without sex.

Chapter 7

The Dynamic Duo: Ruth and Naomi

Ruth and Boaz, a popular biblical love story that focuses on how Ruth trusted God for her Boaz, is often quoted when speaking of celibacy. Although I have no biblical proof, I imagine Ruth, a young woman in her prime, must have endured fear, pain, suffering, and abandonment. Her story is one of great hardship and tragic loss. Having endured lots of mental anguish, fear, abandonment, low self-esteem, depression, anxiety, and physical and mental torment, I imagine Ruth was a hot mess.

Instead of joining a social media group and complaining about how long she was celibate, desperately begging for a Boaz, Ruth literally went to work. She left everything behind, her old way of living and memories of her past life, her family, friends, etc. I have a deep admiration for Ruth, we could have been sisters.

I shared previously that I was with a guy I loved and shared all of my young adult life with. He was all that I'd known regarding love, life, and relationships. On the down side, being in this toxic

47

relationship taught me how to negatively love myself by teaching me to have a lack of value for myself and a lack of boundaries, accepting physical, mental, and verbal abuse. When the relationship ended, I was left alone, confused and afraid, much like I imagine Ruth may have felt when her first husband died. Like Ruth, I needed to rid myself of past memories and experiences in order to collect the new life awaiting me.

Ruth knew she did not have a clue how to live the new life she was being faced with. Instead of being stuck in feelings of grief, abandonment, and hardship, Ruth subconsciously chose Naomi as her mentor to teach her how to live the new life she was presented with. I imagine Naomi, who'd just lost both of her sons, had no idea how to help Ruth. Too old to start over, she was grieving and frustrated. Alone in life, Naomi was experiencing just as much hardship and hopelessness as Ruth. And this is where I feel many women miss the mark, the life changing moment that many of us fail to recognize.

God never intended for anyone to travel through life alone (Genesis 2:18). Our sins, embarrassment, and fear of failure often times cripple us and prevent us from reaching out to mentors or other women who could help us on our journey. I mentioned previously how emptiness on the inside creates an inability to connect with reality and truth. I imagine Ruth asking herself, "Now what? How do I survive this new life?"

Ruth was not worried about sex though. Ruth was focused on survival. For many of us who are celibate, we are focused on finding a man and getting married because we miss sex. It's time we change our focus. Instead of focusing on when we will engage in sex again, we should be more concerned with our survival. Consider this book to be the Naomi to your Ruth, your personal coach, motivator, mentor, and encourager to help heal those inner wounds so you can better love yourself and focus on your survival - living life satisfied without sex.

We know that Ruth decided to stop serving the god of Moab and decided to start serving Naomi's God. While serving her new God, I like to think Ruth began to work on all her inner insecurity issues. The hidden mommy/daddy/childhood traumas, issues of anger, bitterness, or resentment, etc. Many women are celibate, but they are still full of anger, rage, and bitterness.

In this book, you will learn how to be accountable for the mistakes you made that caused you to live a life of hurt, pain, and embarrassment, so you can be content while living celibate. You will learn how to transform from a victim mindset to a victorious mindset. You will be able to identify toxic people and distance yourself from them. Most importantly, you will be able to satisfy yourself without sex.

Chapter 8

First Things First: Love Yourself

Over the years, I was promised by the few men I had sexual encounters with that they were going to reward me with the honor of being their wife. I was led to believe that it was okay to have sex while waiting for their plan to manifest, and if I engaged in sex with them, they would never leave or forsake me. WRONG!

The hard truth was those men did not love me. What was worst, I realized I did not love myself. I thought I did. I had standards, goals, and guidelines. I must have loved myself a little bit, right? I definitely was not a promiscuous girl. I spent the entire decade of 20's with my first sex partner. When it came to my next string of relationships, I followed some of Steve Harvey's advice in regards to the 90-day rule. I offered the men I was in relationships with my support and loyalty. Sometimes I prayed with and for them, so what was my problem? Why was I not good enough for marriage? By the time you enter your 30's unmarried and all of your friends are married, you can't help but question if something is wrong. Why could I not get a guy to marry me?

51

Then I entered the judgement zone, where I started comparing myself to the women around me and the women on social media to determine if I was marriage material or not. For example, this woman has a terrible credit score and wears weave all the time. If she can get married, I know I can get married. As I observed the women in my life, most of them was boastfully having premarital sex. Some of them landed a trip to the altar, some were still playing trial and error. I couldn't imagine a man marrying a woman strictly for sexual pleasures. So I decided to dig deeper into the personal lives of others to understand what landed them a trip down the altar.

Here's what I discovered. I have seen couples who waited until marriage to have sex and couples who had sex before marriage end their marriage. I have seen husbands cheat on their wives. I have seen wives cheat on their husbands. I have seen couples practice open marriage and couples who withhold sex from one another. If marriage was my only goal, there is a 50/50 chance that if I engaged in premarital sex, I would get married.

When I took an even deeper look into the culture of these marriages, some of them got married because they needed a place to stay. Some of got married because they wanted to prove a point to an ex. Some got married because everybody else around them was getting married and they felt it was time for them to get married. Understanding this, I concluded that sex is rarely valued when it comes to getting married. If marriage was based on sexual pleasure alone, then why were so many married people committing adultery? Premarital sex was only half the battle. It's okay to desire marriage, but we should also desire a healthy, godly marriage.

I realized I could have easily married any of the guys I previously dated or had sex with, if only I agreed to provide them with housing, finances, and an endless supply of whatever additional needs that remained unknown.

Most marriages fail because one or both parties are looking for the other person to complete them. God never intended for us to depend on a spouse to complete us. When we do this, that person has become 'God' in our lives. You are depending on this person to supply your needs instead of allowing God to supply your needs. Long story short, we are committing the sin of idolatry. Idolatry is the extreme admiration, love or reverence for someone or something.

During an aha moment, I realized if I was struggling with celibacy, desiring a husband for all the wrong reasons, other Christian women were likely battling the same issue. The objective of the healing phase of this book is for you to grasp that celibacy will not guarantee you a husband, but celibacy will eliminate the NEED to marry a guy and prevent you from committing the sin of idolatry. I like to believe that if you seek first the kingdom of God, through salvation, living in obedience to God, and sharing God's words with others, he will bless you with the desires of your heart (Matthew 6:33). I rejoiced in the fact that God's love for me was greater than the love I had for myself.

If you have purchased this book seeking answers, then you should rejoice too! Rejoice that God rescued you from an abusive relationship. Rejoice that you do not have to financially provide a man's lifestyle for the sake of having a husband. Rejoice that you do not have to pretend on social media that you are happy with your spouse because you were too damaged and broken to believe God has better for you. Rejoice that you do not have to live life with a threatening disease because you chose to stay with a partner who battled from a sex addiction and could not remain faithful. If you are living with a life-threatening disease, rejoice that God is a healer and able to heal you from all mental and physical diseases you may have contracted from being in a toxic relationship. Rejoice!!

Chapter 9

And so, it begins...Healing

In this day and age, premarital sex is the norm. Women and men use sex as an antidepressant, to network, form attachments, for professional advancement in the workplace, as a recreational activity to burn calories to obtain love, or to support their households. Sex can literally be used as a supplement to fill whatever void you need it to fill when you need it.

I believe the undiagnosed culprit of premarital sex and adultery are unhealed trauma, grief, and loss that remains untreated. Most women enter into celibacy because of a broken heart, sexual betrayal or a violation of our sexual right. After many years of loneliness, we then believe our own illusions that we are cured of what hurt us and decide we are ready to start dating again. To our surprise, we end up attracting what we have not healed and the same cycle of abuse is repeated. Then we accuse all men of being dogs and abusers. Another reason premarital sex has become the norm is because sex has been distorted out of the natural context that God intended it to be used.

I initially entered into celibacy because of a broken heart. I did not pursue the necessary healing I needed to be free of soul ties, low self-esteem, or depression. I tried counseling, but I ended up bashing and blaming the guys who hurt me. Don't get me wrong, I was emotionally abused, scarred, traumatized and left spiritually dead by the guys I was involved with, but I knew that approach was not the healing I needed. Yes, it felt good to bash them and their new partners, but I still went home feeling unsatisfied, resenting the women who took my man and appeared to live much happier lives with the same person who was a total monster while dating me.

In some ways, counseling was the foundation that helped me take ownership and accountability for my healing. I researched long and hard to learn how to rid myself of unhealthy emotional and sexual patterns. My Christian experience taught me that if I wanted to be successful regarding the things of God, I had to first renew my mind and reestablish a healthy, firm foundation for myself that would be able to withstand whatever life threw my way. Romans 12:2 (NIV) states, "Do not conform to the pattern of this world, but be transformed by the renewing of your mind. Then you will be able to test and approve what God's will is – his good, pleasing and perfect will."

This is easier said than done. How do you renew your mind when everyone around you are fornicators? I have attended several conferences for singles, women's conference, self-improvement workshops, etc. I'm not here to place blame on anyone, but as for me and my level of comprehension, the information being taught seemed redundant. Women are being taught to not have sex before marriage because of the soul ties that would form, the unwanted pregnancies, the mental disturbances, and

56

the possible infection of sexually transmitted infections We are to fast and pray, pray and fast. It seemed that if I stopped having sex, pray, and fast from something, then I was going to be happy and instantly made whole. I was made to believe that premarital sex was my problem and if I disengaged in sex, disengaged from men, said a prayer and fasted from my most desirable food choice, then I would be renewed.

I believe in fasting and praying, but healing also requires love, approval, security, and survival and I am prepared to share with you all that I've learned while embarking on this journey of self-healing.

Chapter 10

How to be Satisfied without Sex

Before I could be satisfied, I had to identify the ways in which I was unsatisfied and why. By now, we have learned that our weaknesses and insecurities attract toxic people. I had experienced enough heartbreak to know that I no longer wanted to attract another toxic partner. This made me withdraw from men all together. Simultaneously, I experienced internal conflict because I wanted to be "found" by my potential husband who I was sure was out there.

I automatically knew my fear of men was the first order of business I needed to heal. Men in general were not my enemy. For we wrestle not against flesh and blood but against principalities, and against powers, and against the rulers of the darkness of this world (Ephesians 6:12). Therefore, I should not treat men as if they were my enemies, especially since I wanted a man in my life. That which was broken inside of me allowed me to be attracted to the dysfunction that was present in the men catching my attention. Becoming satisfied was an inside job.

During this transition, I journaled, meditated, and prayed for God to give me wisdom to identify what I needed to change about myself. Consider this your self-exploratory session. Write down everything you idolized in a man or the other woman your man left you for. Divide the list into two columns. Column 1) Which of these things do you feel you are able to provide for yourself? Column 2) Which of these things do you feel you need someone else to provide for you? Everything you feel you need a man to provide for you is where your work begins. For example, if you feel you need a man to provide you with a home, income, stability, or a social status, ask God to heal you of your limitations and remove any blockage in your life so that you can become whole. Eliminate the need for this "thing" in your life and focus on your wholeness by providing for yourself the objects you felt a man had to provide for you.

Allow yourself to be vulnerable on paper, let your hand release every inner fears about yourself. After you have written your purest desires, ask God to guide you into how to heal the things you have identified. There were days in this process where I got stuck and didn't know what I needed to fix. Some days, I was in denial about what I wrote. Nobody likes feeling inadequate or admitting that their brokenness is the reason why they may or may not be as successful in picking or attracting the right guy.

After discovering what I needed to heal, I activated my healing by forgiving others and myself for the trauma we caused to my soul. To safeguard myself from any future trauma, I educated myself on boundaries and how to exercise my rights. Healthy relationships are those which require you to make decisions together, foster an environment where you can be open and honest about your feelings with each other, where you feel safe and secure with your partner and you are not afraid of getting hurt. You respect each other's opinions, friends, and interest;

you are able to be yourself and not be compared to an ex, his mother, or other women in his life. You have hobbies and friends outside of your relationship, and the relationship is fun and exciting with mutual respect.

Unhealthy relationships are controlling, consists of dishonesty, physical, mental, and/or emotional abuse, disrespect, sexual abuse, hostility, and creates an environment where you are dependent on your partner for survival. When you set boundaries, you are able to identify these signs of unhealthy relationships early on and have the strength to leave the relationship before things get worse. We teach people how to treat us by what we tolerate. If you tolerate disrespect and dishonesty, that is what will continue. And to think that some women go into marriage with a dishonest, disrespectful man thinking marriage will change his behaviors.

Often times, unhealthy boundaries are learned behavior. From what we observed in our childhood from parents, cousins, best friends, the neighborhoods we grew up in, and the relationships closest to us, we are subconsciously trained on how to conduct a relationship of any scale. For example, as little girl, maybe you observed your mother, an aunt, an older cousin, or a childhood friend involved in a physically or mentally abusive relationship. To make matters worse, they suffered and stayed in this relationship out of "love" or "obligation." Here, you were trained that no matter how a person treats you, you should stay in the relationship out of love and obligation. This example is best understood as generational curses.

Growing up, women in these types of relationships were referred to as the "ride or die chick." Women who could withstand embarrassment and mental and/or physical abuse, tolerate a man's cheating and his multiple babies with multiple women were awarded the prize of being his ride or die chick, which by the way, still does not guarantee you will become his wife. Our lack of boundaries and learned behavior from the previous generation of women we looked up to allowed these types of men to continue entering our lives.

If you are prone to people pleasing, boundary setting can be difficult because you struggle with how people will perceive you. I cared so much about what other people thought of me, I feared if I began setting boundaries for myself, I would lose what little friendships and relationships I thought I had. I established rules and guidelines for myself to override my desire to be a people pleaser.

Observing the trends in my life, I realized that I was the friend anyone could depend on. I was the girlfriend that would stop everything and tend to the needs of my man. I was also loyal to family and strangers. I did this to gain their approval. I could not stand not being accepted by my family, friends, and partners in my life. But if I needed a favor in return, I was made to feel like a burden to the same individuals I'd helped.

It may appear that I am going on and on about boundaries, but this is the most important self-healing technique to rid yourself of toxic relationships and stop attracting toxic partners. If someone has demonstrated a consistent negative behavioral pattern towards you, know that it is not okay to continue tolerating the behavior for the price of having a man, a friendship, or the approval of strangers. Apply this technique to your relationships, friendships, business, and any capacity of your life that involves dealing with people.

Here are a few examples of what boundary setting looks like:

Financially or Materialistically

Financially or materialistically, it means I no longer allow people to borrow money if I am unable to function with that money missing. I would loan out money, neglecting my personal needs, only because I didn't want others to be upset with me. Once that person's payday arrived, I never heard from them, leaving me to feel as if I should have known better than to loan them money. Several weeks to months would go by and I would not hear from this person again until they needed to borrow more money. Without collecting payback on the original loan, I convinced myself this time would be different. The person was in danger of having a car repossessed or getting their lights cut off, and I was convinced they had no other means to get money on such short notice. Once the money was out of my hands, I went back to being ignored. I have since learned that the mismanagement of their funds should not dictate how I manage my funds.

Materialistically, I had to stop associating my self-worth with labels. Better known as a "label whore," name brand or material possessions do not increase your self-esteem or self-worth. It is nice to have nice things, but we should not identify our self-worth by a fancy car or a high priced purse.

Mental Boundaries

This was a huge boundary for me because I cared deeply about the opinions of others regarding my life. I can recall a time someone called me a bad mother because I was advocating for my child in a manner they did not agree with. The statement bothered me for years. In the meantime, this person had no idea how to parent because they were not a parent themselves. They had no idea of the sacrifices I made on a daily basis to make sure my child's needs were met and his safety ensured. I remember feeling foolish for letting this statement ruin how I viewed myself as a parent. I learned that regardless of what other people's opinions of me were, I was doing my best with the resources and education I had been granted. I disconnected from anything that made me mentally feel as if I was less than. Friends, family, associates, strangers, and social media were no longer tolerated in my subconscious.

Another area of mental boundaries I had to establish were my ***personal beliefs and opinions.*** I have had guys try to convince me that it was okay to be promiscuous because they did not care about the amount of sexual partners a woman had, but later they would call a woman a whore if she had several sex partners. There were guys who tried to convince me that their needs came before my children's needs. There were friends who tried to convince me that being celibate meant I must have a sexually transmitted disease or that something was wrong with my vagina. My truth is I believe in God and the power of obedience. I also believe I was blessed because I put my children's needs above my own. Mental boundaries also meant I was able to respect the views and opinions of others without having to compromise my beliefs or engaging in a heated debate.

Physical Boundaries

Physical boundaries meant I would no longer allow a guy to place his hands on me in a manner that I felt was abusive. I also determined simple guidelines to control my celibacy. Was I going to give out hugs from an angle or was it better to exchange a handshake or wave? Do I have conversations with the opposite sex after dark or should I only communicate with them during the day? I stopped inviting people into my personal space, my home and I chose to not be alone with certain people in private areas. Being alone meant I was more susceptible to vulnerability, and it was easy for me to be manipulated. I opted for public places where others are around if I were on a date or doing a meet and greet with a guy, nothing intimate such as a parked car in or a tucked away corner of a nearly empty restaurant.

Emotional Boundaries

Setting *emotional boundaries* for me was to disengage from other people's problems. Their problems were not my problems. Their emergency was not my emergency. If you mismanaged your money for the month, it was not my responsibility to solve your financial problem. I was no longer obligated to be a personal therapist to friends and/or family who habitually practiced bad decision making, particularly for those who were unavailable to lend me a shoulder to lean on or allow me sixty minutes to vent about my problems.

Sexual Boundaries

I would no longer hide my celibacy for the sake of attracting a man. I would no longer break my celibacy for the sake of having a temporary relationship. I would no longer engage in sex because I did not want to be alone. I took a vow to get to know myself. To heal all inner voids, wounds, emotional, mental, and spiritual issues, so that the decisions I made were not based on sexual emotions. I would no longer allow someone else's views on celibacy prevent me from being satisfied without sex.

Setting boundaries was the blueprint to a healthy relationship with myself and others. Several times people pleasing got the best of me and I experienced guilt and resentment, which morphed into anger that I spewed onto others because someone had to pay for contributing to the abuse I allowed others to perform on me. It was awkward at first to tell someone no I would not lend them money. Or no, they could not come to my home and chill. No, I was unavailable to give them a ride or fix their crisis. Several relationships ended when I began to firmly practice my boundaries. But a very important relationship was birthed, a relationship with me.

Healing Abandonment Issues

Before we can begin to heal our abandonment issues, we must identify the root cause of the abandonment. Often times, when a person lacks the physical and psychological protection that is needed to reduce fear and anxiety, abandonment issues are formed. This can birth from lack of protection from your parents or lack of protection from a first love or someone you deeply trusted who betrayed your trust. When a person is repeatedly exposed to acts of abandonment, it can lead to mental issues such as post-traumatic stress disorder, severe depression, isolation, social anxiety, low self-esteem or lack of self-worth.

I dreaded being alone. I hated eating alone. I hated spending quiet time with myself. I made the excuse that I did not have enough money to enjoy an adventurous life. I used my children as an excuse for being stuck in the house. I quickly realized I needed to heal this fear of being alone. Perhaps being afraid to be alone was actually fear of abandonment. But why did I feel this way?

Being with my first love was a euphoric experience that was indescribable and hard to put into words. I was addicted to him and felt sick when we were apart. The first time we seriously broke up, I stayed inside all day and night, sleeping my life away hoping I was in the middle of a bad dream. Over time, the constant break up to make up created an environment where I felt safe when he was around and felt as if I couldn't survive when he was gone, regardless of how physically or verbally abusive he was.

I later realized our bond was built off trauma. Trauma Bonding, which some may refer to as soul ties, is a repeated, consistent, intentional act of physical and emotional abuse that the abuser illustrates through the acts of reward and punishment to create an emotional bond or stronghold that leaves the victim believing they need their abuser in order to survive. The victim becomes addicted and attached to the abuse, making it difficult to leave the abuser. Trauma bonding can be learned as a child. If you were raised in an environment where violence and abuse regularly occurred, a child can grow up believing this is normal behavior and will be unable to distinguish between a healthy and unhealthy relationship. This is the perfect environment to attract psychopaths and narcissist.

Psychopaths are destructive uncaring individuals who lack empathy, are irresponsible, and have a high sense of self-worth and selfishness. These individuals have an inability to plan for the future, can be easily bored or inattentive, and can be physically or verbally violent. Psychopaths are attractive to individuals who lack boundaries, who have a high sense of empathy towards other. Individuals who are codependent and like to feel responsible for the happiness of others; Introverts who can be viewed as loners or someone who do not have a lot of friends; older women who are financially stable with a good job, car, and house; single mothers who may need a father figure to their child(ren) are all likely to be potential prey for a psychopath.

A psychopath's goal is to idealize, devalue, and discard their victims. The idealize phase is often the period of time where they gaslight their victim. You are led to believe that you are the best thing that ever happened to them and the relationship is a godsend. Once you are hooked by the constant love bombing, you begin to enter the devalue phase. This is where you are led to believe that everything is your fault. Maybe if you lose ten pounds, he wouldn't cheat on you anymore. Maybe if you supply all of his financial needs, he wouldn't have to date other women outside the relationship to get his financial needs met. Once you are discarded, you are left with feelings of emptiness as he moves on to a newer, prettier, younger or older woman who has made it seem like she is better than you.

These types of relationships leave you with fear of rejection. Fear of living alone. Fear of trusting again. Often times, women isolate themselves from others and suffer privately from depression and trauma unaware that they were victims of this type of abuse. Often times, these victims appear guarded and closed off, unable to attract and connect to healthy relationships because of their addiction to trauma bonding.

It is never too late to avoid a toxic relationship or get out of one and I believe we can do this by establishing an accountability partner.

It is impossible to be accountable when you do not have anyone to challenge you into your growth. I knew I needed a support system to help me be accountable. Previously, I deprived myself of a support system by withdrawing from my family and friends out of embarrassment. I was embarrassed to keep going back to the same man who hurt me after I had told all of my family and friends how he continuously hurt me. Without having a proper support system to act as your accountability team, it is easy to fall prey to psychopaths, narcissists, and manipulators.

As stated earlier, Genesis 2:18 identifies that it is not good for man to be alone. I'd like to think this does not only apply to obtaining a husband or a wife, but also to business relationships, friendships, partnerships, etc. Often times, our loneliness can be avoided simply by picking up the phone and calling a friend or family member.

In this new entrepreneurial age, everyone is willing to be a coach or accountability partner for a small fee. I have nothing against those type of partnerships if you can afford it. Sometimes, the business relationship can turn into a genuine friendship and you may not be required to pay for the services being rendered from a "friend." The benefit of paying for an accountability partner is the freedom from judgment you may experience if you shared your problems, goals, or dreams, with a family member or friend.

My sister serves as my accountability partner. She is like my human diary. I'm not here to persuade anyone to purchase accountability services, there are free and low cost options available for you. Social media has several groups dedicated to being celibate and healing from traumatic relationships but proceed with caution when you enter some of these group as people from all different stages of healing are allowed to participate and most moderators are not mental health professionals or licensed therapists. You will want to avoid groups that engage in bashing ex-partners, placing blame, or importance on the length of time you have been celibate.

After years and years of trying to demand love and receive love from men who made me feel unworthy, my self-esteem was the next order of business in my healing journey. Why did I connect my self-worth to what people did or didn't do for me? When you idolize others, you relinquish your power of self. You allow yourself to be manipulated and find yourself performing to obtain their desired result.

Low self-esteem may also result from an incident that happened during your childhood. Perhaps you were bullied in school, grew up in an abusive household, were violated as a child, or abandoned by a parent, these types of events subconsciously reflect on how we see ourselves.

Because you were abandoned by your father, you settle for a man of any capacity simply to have a man around. If your parents told you would never amount to anything, you feel as if having a man will prove them wrong and give you the social status you long for.

We can increase our self-worth and self-esteem by identifying who we are in Christ. How do we do this? 2 Corinthians 5:17 teaches us that if anyone is in Christ, they are a new creation and the old has gone away. We learn that we are accepted in Christ through friendship, being a child of God, being justified, united in his Love and Spirit, a member of his body with direct access to God through his Holy Spirit, redeemed and made complete in him.

We are secure in Christ, free from condemnation, with the assurance that all things will work together for our good. We are citizens of heaven and nothing can separate us from the love of God. We are free from the condemning charges against us and we can find grace and mercy in our time of need.

You are significant in Christ because you are the salt and life of the earth, appointed and anointed to be a witness of Christ. You are God's ambassador and you are able to approach him with freedom and confidence with the ability to do all things through Christ who strengthens you. Lastly but not least, you are never alone. God will never leave or forsake you. As you begin to see yourself as God sees you, recite who the bible says you are in Christ. Your self-worth, self-esteem, and self-confidence will greatly improve! Use this model to measure all relationships in your life and disconnect from anyone who sees you less than how God sees you.

We've learned that the lack of psychological protection stemming from childhood or introduced through a toxic relationship can lead to a fear of abandonment. That fear of abandonment creates trauma bonds/soul ties and additions to unhealthy relationships. Healing begins when we forgive ourselves for the role we played in the abuse, set boundaries, and remain accountable through an accountability partner, support groups, or therapy. To prevent any future relapses, become aware of your personal abandonment triggers and set boundaries. Identify what makes you hurt. Is it a song? A location? Holidays? Be intentional about creating boundaries and develop a plan for how you are going to spend your time to avoid replaying hurtful events.

Educate yourself on psychopaths / narcissists / manipulators to quickly identify toxic patterns in friendships and relationships and not form bonds with these types of individuals.

Chapter 11

The Fifth Year Struggle — Understanding God's Grace and Mercy.

When I decided I wanted to write about this topic on how to help others be satisfied without sex, I came across several women who also struggled in their fifth year of abstinence. Here is a quick re-cap of my first five-year journey with celibacy:

My first year abstaining from sex, I was a part of an awesome bible-based church. I was reintroduced to Jesus and learned about him in a way that made me crave to know more about him. I started volunteering in the church, attending women's conferences, singles' events, bible study, you name it. I was excited to share with others how God was blessing me and strengthening me in my celibacy walk.

The second year was a breeze. I stayed focused and faithful to my beliefs. Even though I missed my ex-boyfriend and missed hanging out and doing things with other people my age, I stayed away from them because I didn't want to be tempted by my old life. I isolated myself from individuals, places, events, and even music that reminded me of my past life. The women in the church were cool, but most of them were married or single without children, so I couldn't really connect with them because I didn't have a babysitter and couldn't afford to hang out. This was a pretty lonely year for me, but I continued to follow my routine, attending conferences, church every Sunday, bible study every Wednesday. I figured staying busy was best to avoid being lonely.

My third year abstaining from sex, I was hopeful my faithfulness would eventually pay off. A few single women I was acquainted with were getting engaged and it seemed as if women who had abstained from sex for only a few months were meeting the guy of their dreams and getting married within a matter of months. This was around the time Ciara and Russell Wilson started dating. Ciara was in a relationship with a famous rapper, had a baby by him, and he cheated on her. She left the relationship while her baby was only a few months old and started dating a famous football player. The couple claimed to have abstained from sex during the entire friendship/dating phase and would eventually get married and have more children. Follow them on social media if you haven't already. Then actress Megan Good married her husband, Devon Franklin. They share with the world how Megan was only celibate for less than a year and boom! God blessed her with the man of her dreams.

Well into my third year, all of this was very encouraging. I figured things had to be coming around for me. I was a single parent desperately seeking a father figure for my son who was beginning to act out in school, and I had no idea on how to raise a boy or address the issues he was experiencing.

Entering into my fourth year of abstinence, I was frustrated. Even non-celibate folks were getting engaged and married, and I was thinking, what is the point of this thing? Why do I have to abstain from sex and here are Christians, fornicating, still going to church, and still getting married to what appears to be pretty decent men? My frustration impacted my church attendance. I felt like the only guys at my church were already married, in committed relationships or too old for me. I enjoyed the pastor and the church as a whole, but I needed to branch out and visit other locations in hopes of meeting a man.

By year five, my life was in shambles. The company I was working for was stealing money from the employees, which forced me to quit. I was having family problems with my siblings. My son was exhibiting negative behavior, and I was depressed, lonely, and pretending to everyone around me that things were *okay*. I was done being alone. I needed the help of a man. So I did what I knew to do, I found me a man.

Anytime you go outside the will of God, you have to stay outside of the will of God in order to maintain what you obtained. It wasn't long before I was having sex again in order to maintain my ungodly relationship with this guy. Truth of the matter was, I knew this guy was trouble. I felt in my spirit that he was not the one. I distanced myself from my family because I wanted to avoid having the "so when are we going to meet him?" conversation.

Here is what I found significant about the fifth year struggle. The number five is the biblical number for God's grace. God's grace is his goodness towards humanity regardless of our actions. This divine favor is given to us because God loves us. Grace is not to be confused with merit. Merit is the quality of being good or worthy of a reward, punishment, or attention. To sum this up, regardless of the good or bad we have done in our lives, sometimes God blesses us because of his grace. But if we live out his commandments, identify and stay in his will for our lives, then we will be rewarded by his merit for doing what he told us to do.

So what does this have to do with the fifth year struggle? In any relationship, job, marriage, or task that you have set out to complete, you may look back and realize the fifth year was always the make or break year. It is the year you will either thrive or fall apart. Years one through three are traditionally your foundational years. These are the years you learn and establish order. Note my first year of celibacy, I was on fire and excited to learn all I could to be successful during this journey.

Year four was my year of complacency. I thought I knew everything I needed to know about success with celibacy. I stopped educating myself and grew comfortable in staying stagnant and eventually became distracted by focusing on everybody else's journey. I should have used this time to continue growing and healing. By year five, I was frustrated and gave in to my temptation. I was expecting God to reward my time of being celibate with a husband and I was tired of being alone.

That experience taught me, "...Suffering produces perseverance; perseverance, character; and character, hope. And hope does not put us to shame..." (Romans 5:4-5). I fell short because I was not focused on building my character as a celibate woman. I was more focused on the reward of getting a husband instead of healing the void in my life caused by broken and abusive relationships, low self-esteem, and the fear of being lonely. This is what I believe is the foundation of success to "Ciara's Prayer."

76

This explains why some women can be celibate for two weeks and meet and marry a man in seven days while others can be celibate for ten to twenty years and grow frustrated each year as they acknowledge another year of being single and sexless. There are some women who may never marry because that is not God's plan for your life. We must not look at celibacy as a punishment or as a means to be rewarded a husband if we live out this assignment, but rather a form of obedience, to honor God with our bodies.

Chapter 12

What does godly dating look like?
The codes and ethics of
dating while celibate

It is important to know that you are not single as an act of punishment from God. And it doesn't necessarily mean that you are severely broken inside. It also doesn't mean you are 100% perfect and have nothing to worry about. No matter where you are on your journey, God is still preparing you emotionally, spiritually, and mentally so that the generational curses in your family is not lived out in your marriage or your children. To begin this phase of preparation for godly dating, we will start with what love looks like.

When I think of the perfect love, I think of 1 Corinthians 13:4-8: ***"Love is patient, love is kind. It does not envy, it does not boast, it is not proud. It does not dishonor others, it is not self-seeking, it is not easily angered, it keeps no record of wrongs. Love does not delight in evil but rejoices with the truth."***

It is said that when you are dating or considering marrying a guy, you should replace his name in every spot where you see the word love. For example; Andre is patient. Andre is kind. Andre does not envy and Andre is not boastful... This is a good model to pray for your future husband, that he possess these qualities before you meet him. For some, the ultimate goal of dating is to find a life partner. In doing so, 1 Corinthians 10:31 says that everything we do should be done to glorify God, relationships included.

Now that we have identified and healed our hidden traumas, built our self-esteem and self-worth, thrown off our old baggage of sins and bad habits according to Ephesians 4:22-24, we are mentally healthy and ready to begin dating again. It's important that we learn what godly dating looks like so we do not fall into the trap of fornication or dysfunctional dating.

We can glorify God in our relationships by dating according to God's will. But first, we have to identify what a godly man looks like. Please understand, no man is perfect. He may come with a few flaws, but his overall qualities should be good, honorable, God-fearing, strong in his faith, and wants to pursue and love you as Christ loves the church. These types of men will take their time to get to know you in a healthy manner. He will not be controlling or verbally or mentally abusive. They will not mislead you, play games, or give you an emotional run around. He will be gentle and compassionate with you and empathetically in-tune with you. He will want to develop a friendship first and will be interested in spiritual intimacy rather than physical intimacy. A godly man will be intentional about his plan, God's plan and your plans. His value is not placed in material possessions. A relationship with him will be purposeful, honest, patient, and protected. A godly man will exercise self-control, be filled with wisdom, and remain faithful to you. He is a provider and a peacemaker. Isn't that exciting? I suggest highlighting this paragraph and using this model to pray for your godly husband.

Here is my chronological interpretation of what godly dating looks like. Second Corinthians 6:14-15 says it is not wise to date someone who does not love God, better known as do not be unequally yoked. If a Christian relationship is what you are after, it is best to date a Christian.

Most everyone you meet now-a-days professes to be a Christian. The bible gives Christians specific instructions on how you should live a Christian life and one of those is to not engage in premarital sex. If you meet a man who possess other Godly qualities but struggles with abstaining from sex, continue to pray for him that he discovers his identity in Christ before you enter into a relationship with him. Entering into a relationship with him before he establishes his relationship with Christ can be a messy combination filled with temptation. Stay away from individuals who are abusive, manipulative, a drunkard, practices idolatry, or those who have a bad temper. Most of this can be found in 1 Corinthians 5:11. An ideal partner, according to Philippians 2:1-2, looks like someone with good character, who encourages you and supports you and has the qualities found in 1 Timothy 3. Stay away from individuals who are evil and give off evil thoughts (see 2 Timothy 2:22).

It is still important to maintain physical, mental, and spiritual boundaries while dating the godly way. Proverbs 4:23 teaches us to guard your heart because it determines the course of your life. We, women, should continue to be our best selves, developing good character, setting goals and meeting them. When you stop setting goals, you become complacent. Coasting through with nothing to do. We should continue to seek God and identify what the next plan is for our life. Volunteer, help and serve others, and pray for your future spouse.

While dating, it is also important for women to be interdependent and self-sufficient, while still needing masculinity in her life. To be interdependent means to be dependent upon each other, relying on each other for survival. The problem is women are being trained not to need a man. Once you have been single for a very long time, it is easy to fall into this strong, independent, bossy mindset of not needing a man. Women do need men and that reason is deeper than sex. I believe that remaining vulnerable to this need while identifying our purpose and identity is part of the secret to attracting a man who has established his identity and purpose. The bible teaches us in Genesis 2:18 that it is not good for man to be alone.

When God created Adam and Eve, he created two separate, wholesome individuals. Galatians 3:27-28 teaches there is no distinction or preference between man and woman because we are all one in Jesus Christ. Simply put, a man does not complete a woman, but we must be careful not to operate in masculine roles to the point where we do not place value on the role a man plays in our lives. Men need to feel wanted in a healthy manner, not manipulated or forced to help.

If you have been single for a long time, practice being interdependent by asking others for help when you truly need help. Develop yourself by identifying your personal life's mission and goals you are passionate about. Doing so creates your own identity and gives you a foundation to stand firm on so that your mission, purpose, goals and dreams are not constantly changing with every new relationship you enter.

When you've identified these things for yourself, you are able to recognize a man who is not able to survive independently by himself. Rather he is interdependently depending on a relationship with woman in order to survive. Be careful not to confuse this with manipulation and control. A man's need for a woman should not isolate you from family or friends or strip you of your identity. This is not an example of a healthy relationship. Your role as a woman is to not take care of the man you are dating. You can encourage him according to 1 Thessalonians 5:11, "Therefore encourage one another and build one another up, just as you're doing."

Do not fall prey to building a man up and waiting for him to become marriage material. This will create regret and bitterness after he has finally gotten himself together and then leaves you and marries another woman. It is not your job to raise a man.

Knowing when to terminate a relationship is crucial to the dating process. In the past, you may have experienced toxic relationships where you held on and gave multiple chances in hopes of this person changing their negative ways. What that did was tell your partner how much abuse you were willing to tolerate. It is time to terminate a relationship when negative and abusive behaviors that were not present at the beginning of the relationship appear more frequently, when power struggles are formed, or if you or your partner are experiencing excessive boredom in the relationship. Other red flags to be mindful of include misunderstandings that escalate to violence, rage, physical or mental abuse or when it appears the mask has been dropped and he is a different person than he was when you first met him. There could be several reasons why a relationship may need to end, but these are a few definite deal breakers that signify a potentially toxic relationship.

Give yourself enough time to date a guy so that negative signs can present itself. As always, allow the voice of God to lead you in or out of a relationship. Do not rush to get to the altar. Instead, enjoy learning and growing with your partner while maintaining your celibacy. When necessary, attend couples counseling before getting married and continue setting goals for the relationship and marriage to continue growing with your partner.

Most importantly, know that celibacy does not guarantee you a husband. Sexual purity should be viewed as an image of your relationship with God. Your true and proper worship to God is to offer your bodies as a living sacrifice per Romans 12:1. 1 Corinthians 6:18 teaches us that whoever commits sexual sins, commit sins against their own body and 1 Peter 2:11 teaches us that this wages war against your own soul. For the pure in heart will see God according to Matthew 5:8.

About the Author

Latonya Jones has been independently motivating, encouraging, and supporting women through toxic and abusive relationships for several years. Her educational background, including a master's degree in Human Service and bachelor's degree in Journalism, has led her to blog on social media platforms that focus on parenting, family matters, and mental health awareness. Her humanitarian efforts can be confirmed through her support group, Nattalicious, where she collects hair care products and toiletry items through the Stuff-A-Purse campaign to distribute to local women's shelters. She has worked as a mental health professional and provided case management service for several social service agencies. You may learn more about her work as a human service professional by visiting www.latonyajones.com

Made in the USA
Middletown, DE
06 January 2023

21499588R00055